SHEHRAJ SINGH

Naval's Wisdom on Wealth & Business

Contents

Preface

I have been obsessed with Naval and his philosophy on business, wealth, money, startups, and health.

Over the years, I have been reading his tweets, and decoding them, and Eric Jorgenson, along with many other bloggers, has made a significant impact by explaining novel concepts to me. This book is a continuation of that idea.

I picked up Naval's quotes from the internet that I truly admire and that resonated with me daily. Me and ChatGPT, wrote a summary, simply explaining those concepts. You can read it to gain insights.

Each chapter in the book features one quote and its explanation. If you purchase this book, you can open any page on any day of the year, read the content, and quickly learn the theory behind it.

This is the simple idea behind the book, something I desired. I created it, and now it's available on the web. I hope you guys like it. Thank you so much.

1

No one can compete with you on being you

No one can compete with you on being you. Most of life is a search for who and what needs you the most.

No one can ever beat you at being yourself. Just think about it - there's no one out there who can replicate your unique combination of thoughts, experiences, and perspectives. You are truly one of a kind.

When it comes to finding meaning in life, it's all about figuring out who and what truly depends on you. It's not about trying to impress everyone or chase after every opportunity. Instead, focus on understanding where your presence and contributions are most needed. What do you bring to the table that no one else can?

This quote reminds us that there is something special about each of us, and we have a responsibility to discover and share it with the world. Life becomes much more fulfilling when we prioritize this search for purpose and connection, rather than constantly trying to fit into someone else's mold or chasing superficial measures of success.

So take a moment to embrace your individuality and reflect on who truly needs you in their life. It could be a friend, a family member, a cause, or even a community. Remember, the biggest impact you can make is by being authentically you and offering your unique gifts to those who truly appreciate them.

2

Startups are hard. Every time I forget, reality slaps me upside the head.

Startups are tough. It's easy to get caught up in the excitement and forget about the hardships that come along with it.

But reality has a funny way of bringing us back down to earth. It reminds us that building a successful startup takes more than just a great idea or a lot of hard work. It requires resilience, determination, and a willingness to face challenges head-on. So when things get tough, and they will, remember that this is all part of the game.

Embrace the challenges as opportunities for growth and learning. Don't let temporary setbacks discourage you. Keep pushing forward, stay focused on your goals, and remember why you started this journey in the first place. The road to success is never easy, but if you can navigate through the ups and downs, the rewards can be truly life-changing. So buckle up, because the journey is just beginning.

3

Learn to sell. Learn to build. If you can do both, you will be unstoppable.

When it comes to success, there are two essential skills that you need to master: selling and building.

- Selling refers to the ability to persuade and influence others, to communicate your ideas effectively and convince them of your value.
- Building, on the other hand, is about creating and constructing something of value, whether it's a business, a product, or a relationship.

The reason why learning to sell and build is so important is because these two skills go hand in hand. You can be the best builder in the world, but if you can't effectively sell your ideas or products, they won't gain the recognition they deserve. Conversely, being a great salesperson won't get you far if you can't back up your words with a solid foundation of what you're selling.

By learning to sell, you become a master at connecting with others, understanding their needs, and persuading them to see the value in what you have to offer. This skill allows you to build relationships, secure partnerships, and ultimately grow your influence.

On the other hand, learning to build equips you with the ability to create some-thing valuable and meaningful. By focusing on developing your skills, creating a strong foundation, and consistently improving, you lay the groundwork for long-term success.

When you combine these two essential skills of selling and building, you become an unstoppable force. You have the power to bring your ideas to life, attract opportunities, and achieve your goals.

Selling and building complement each other in a powerful way. When you can effectively sell, you can communicate the value of what you've built and convince others to support or invest in it. You can build a network of loyal customers, clients, and collaborators who believe in your vision and are eager to be part of your success.

Likewise, when you have strong building skills, you can create something that people want and need. You can develop innovative products or services that solve problems or fulfill desires.

4

Money does buy happiness, if you earned it.

Simply having money does not guarantee happiness, but if you have worked hard and put in the effort to earn that money, it can bring a sense of fulfillment and satisfaction.

When you earn money through your own hard work and perseverance, it becomes a symbol of your achievements and the value you have provided to others. It represents the impact you have made in the world and the value you have created for yourself and those around you. This is why earning money can bring a sense of purpose and happiness.

On the other hand, if you simply inherit or win a large sum of money without having put in the effort to earn it, it may not bring the same level of satisfaction or happiness. Money earned through your own endeavors carries a deeper meaning and sense of accomplishment.

So, the big idea behind this quote is that the process of earning money, rather than just having money, is what brings true happiness. It is the journey, the challenges overcome, and the growth experienced along the way that make the rewards of money meaningful.

5

If you want to be wealthy, spend your time earning, learning, or relaxing. Outsource or ignore everything else.

If you want to build wealth, focus on the activities that directly contribute to earning money, expanding your knowledge, or taking time to rest and recharge. Everything else that doesn't fall into these categories, either delegate it to others or simply let it go.

Spending your time on these three key areas allows you to maximize your potential for financial growth.

- By actively earning, whether through your work or investments, you are generating income that can compound over time.
- Learning new skills and knowledge expands your capabilities, making you more valuable in the marketplace and increasing your earning potential.
- Relaxation and self-care - taking time to rest and recharge allows you to maintain your focus and energy, ensuring that you can perform at your best.

By prioritizing these activities and minimizing your focus on things that don't directly contribute to your financial goals, you are maximizing your efficiency and setting yourself up for long-term success. It's all about making conscious choices about where and how you invest your time, with the intention of creating wealth and a fulfilling life.

6

Optimize for control over money, and you'll make more money

By reading this quote, I've come to realize that if you want to make more money, it's important to prioritize control over it. By control, I mean having the power to make decisions and influence how your money is managed. When you have control, you can protect and grow your wealth.

Think about it - when you don't have control, you are at the mercy of others. You have to rely on someone else to make decisions on your behalf, which often leads to unfavorable outcomes. Whether it's entrusting your money to a financial advisor or investing in someone else's business, you are essentially giving up control over your hard-earned money.

On the other hand, when you prioritize control, you are in the driver's seat. You can choose where and how to invest your money, ensuring that it aligns with your goals and values. You have the freedom to take calculated risks and make adjustments whenever necessary. This level of control gives you the potential to make more money because you have the power to make strategic decisions that are in your best interest.

So, if you want to maximize your financial success, focus on gaining and maintaining control over your money. Take the time to educate yourself, build financial literacy, and make informed decisions. By doing so, you

7

Escape competition through authenticity

Playing long-term games with long-term people means that instead of constantly trying to outdo others or compete with them, you focus on building authentic and genuine relationships with people who have the same mindset. Instead of short-term gains and quick wins, you prioritize long-term growth and success.

This idea applies not only to business but to all aspects of life. When you invest in long-term relationships, whether it's with business partners, colleagues, or friends, you create a foundation of trust and mutual respect. These relationships become a source of compound interest, where the value and benefits grow over time.

In business, being trustworthy and having a good reputation are crucial. When you consistently show integrity, deliver on your promises, and build a solid reputation, people will trust and respect you. This trust compounds over time, leading to more opportunities and success.

The same principle applies to personal relationships. When you have strong, long-term relationships with people who share your values and goals, the little conflicts and negotiations that often arise in relationships become easier to navigate. You trust each other, and you know that no matter what challenges arise, you will work through them together.

The big idea behind this quote is to prioritize authenticity, integrity, and long-term thinking in your relationships. By doing so, you can escape the cutthroat competition and create a foundation of trust and growth that will benefit you in all areas of life.

8

What you want in life is to be in control of your time. You want to get into a leveraged job where you control your own time and you're tracked on the outputs.

The key to having control over our time and achieving true freedom lies in finding a leveraged job. In a leveraged job, we have the power to control our own time and the focus is on the results we deliver, rather than the number of hours we put in.

Imagine being able to work smarter, not harder, and still have the ability to make a significant impact. That's the beauty of a leveraged job. It allows us to maximize our productivity and prioritize the things that truly matter to us.

When we're focused on outputs instead of inputs, we can create a work-life balance that suits our needs. We can structure our days in a way that aligns with our personal goals and responsibilities. We can have the freedom to spend more time with our loved ones, pursue our passions, and take care of our well-being.

So, if you want to take charge of your time and live life on your own terms, it's time to seek out a leveraged job. Don't settle for being chained to a traditional 9-5 job that consumes all your time and energy. Instead, aim for a career that allows you to leverage your skills and expertise, giving you the flexibility and freedom you crave.

Remember, life is too short to be stuck in a job that controls your time. Take the leap, find a leveraged job, and start living life on your own terms. The power to control your time is in your hands, so don't wait any longer to make a change.

9

Meetings are the death of productivity

No meetings before 11am. No meetings when emails or calls will do. Don't schedule calls, text coordinate them on the fly when possible. Cram all meetings into two days a week. 1-on-1s are usually 30-minute walking meetings. (Meetings are the death of productivity)

Meetings can be a major drain on productivity. By limiting the number of meetings you have and structuring them efficiently, you can free up more time for focused work.

Scheduling meetings after 11am allows you to have uninterrupted time in the morning to tackle important tasks and set your priorities for the day. This way, you can dive into your work without distractions and get things done.

10

If someone can train other people how to do something, then they can replace you.

If someone can train other people how to do something, then they can replace you. If they can replace you, then they don't have to pay you a lot. You want to know how to do something other people don't know how to do at the time period when those skills are in demand.

If you want to be valued and paid well, you need to have skills that are in demand and not easily replaceable. It's simple logic - if someone else can do what you do, then they can be hired instead of you, which means you have less bargaining power when it comes to your salary.

The key is to have a unique set of skills that are valuable and difficult to reproduce. This could be expertise in a specific field, proficiency in a certain technology or software, or mastery of a particular craft. By staying ahead of the curve and constantly learning new things, you ensure that you have something of value to offer that sets you apart from others.

In today's rapidly changing world, the demand for certain skills is constantly evolving. So, it's important to stay curious, adaptable, and always be on the lookout for opportunities to learn and grow. By constantly developing and honing your skills, you position yourself as an indispensable asset in any industry or profession. And when you're invaluable, you have the leverage to negotiate better compensation for your work.

11

Rich people get paid by the project and pay by the hour

One of the biggest differences between rich and poor people is how they think about time and money.

Rich people understand the power of leverage - they aim to get paid by the project, where they can earn a large amount of money for a single task, rather than being paid by the hour, where their income is limited by the number of hours they can work.

When you get paid by the project, you have the opportunity to earn exponentially more because you can optimize your time and skills to deliver exceptional results. You're not stuck trading your hours for a fixed wage. Instead, you focus on creating value that can have a lasting impact.

On the other hand, poor people often trade their time for money. They get stuck in a cycle of trading hours for wages, which can limit their financial growth. The real wealth lies in finding ways to leverage your time and skills to create value and get paid accordingly.

So, if you want to break free from the constraints of trading time for money, start thinking about how you can get paid by the project, where your income potential is not limited by the number of hours you work.

12

Easy choices, hard life. Hard choices, easy life.

> Like everything in life, if you are willing to make the short-term sacrifice, you'll have the long-term benefit. 'Easy choices, hard life. Hard choices, easy life.'

If you're constantly looking for quick wins and immediate gratification, you're setting yourself up for a hard life.

You might get some temporary happiness in the moment, but in the long run, you'll find yourself stuck in the same place, without any lasting progress. On the other hand, if you're willing to put in the hard work and make difficult choices that align with your long-term goals, you'll have an easier life in the end.

Sure, it's not always fun or easy in the present moment, but the compound effect of your efforts will pay off exponentially over time.

Stop chasing instant gratification and start playing the long game. Make choices that will yield long-term benefits, even if they're not the easiest or most comfortable. Trust me, it'll be worth it in the end.

13

Solve via iteration. Then get paid via repetition.

When it comes to solving problems or achieving goals, the key is to keep iterating. Don't expect to find the perfect solution right away. Instead, take small steps, learn from them, make adjustments, and repeat the process. It's through this iterative approach that you can refine your methods and ultimately find success.

But solving problems is just the first step. To actually benefit from your solutions, you need to put them into action repeatedly. Repetition is essential for creating value and getting rewarded for your efforts. Consistently applying your solutions, whether it's in business, relationships, or personal growth, allows you to build a track record of success. It's by proving yourself over time that you gain credibility and earn opportunities for greater rewards.

```
Don't expect instant gratification or immediate success. Embrace
the power of iteration and repetition to steadily progress towards
your goals and ultimately reap the benefits.
```

14

If you can buy happiness, buy it

If you can buy happiness, buy it. Sometimes, we get caught up in thinking that money can't buy happiness. But the truth is, there are certain things that money can buy that can make us happy.

It could be treating yourself to a vacation, buying your dream car, or even just having the financial freedom to do what you love. Of course, money alone won't bring everlasting happiness, but it can contribute to it.

So, if you have the means to buy something that brings you joy, go ahead and do it. Don't feel guilty or ashamed for wanting to spend money on your happiness. Sometimes, buying experiences or things that bring us joy can be a valuable investment in our overall well-being.

So, if you can afford it, why not make the purchase and enjoy the happiness it brings?

15

If you don't own a piece of a business, you don't have a path towards financial freedom

If you don't own a part of a business, you won't have a clear way to achieve financial freedom. Sure, you can work a regular job and earn a salary, but that alone won't give you the opportunity to truly build wealth and have control over your financial future.

Being a business owner means you have the potential for exponential growth. By owning a piece of a business, you have the chance to benefit from the power of compounding. As the business grows and becomes more successful, the value of your ownership stake increases. This growth can create wealth and provide you with the financial freedom you desire.

On the other hand, if you're solely dependent on a salary, your income is limited. You're trading time for money, and there's a cap to how much you can earn. Plus, you don't have the same level of control and influence over your financial destiny.

So, if you truly want financial freedom, it's important to consider owning a piece of a business as a path towards achieving that goal. It's about finding opportunities to invest in businesses or starting your own and harnessing the power of compounding to build and grow your wealth.

16

The purpose of wealth is freedom

Wealth should not be seen as an end goal or a status symbol, but rather as a means to live life on your own terms.

When you have wealth, you have the freedom to make choices without being constrained by financial limitations. You can pursue your passions, spend time with loved ones, travel, and live a life of abundance and fulfillment.

However, it's important to remember that wealth is not just about financial riches, but also about having time, health, and meaningful relationships. True wealth is about achieving a well-rounded sense of freedom and happiness in all areas of life.

17

You won't have inner peace until you give up your war against the world

It's important to realize that happiness and inner peace don't come from constantly fighting against the world. We often get caught up in trying to control everything around us, trying to make things go the way we want them to. But this constant struggle only brings stress and frustration.

The big idea here is that true inner peace can only be found when we let go of our need to control and accept the world as it is. Instead of waging a war against the world, we should focus on finding peace within ourselves. This means accepting that there will always be things beyond our control, and learning to let go of our attachment to outcomes.

When we stop fighting against the world and start embracing it with all its imperfections, we can find a sense of peace and contentment. So, instead of constantly resisting and struggling, try to surrender to the flow of life and find peace within yourself.

18

I would love to be paid purely for my judgment, not for any work. I want a robot, capital, or computer to do the work, but I want to be paid for my judgment

The big idea behind this quote is the desire for intellectual capital and the value of one's judgment. It suggests that the ultimate goal is to be in a position where you are compensated solely for making high-quality decisions and providing valuable insights, rather than just for the work itself.

This implies a vision of reaching a level where one's expertise and experience command a premium, allowing for more autonomous and strategic decision-making. It highlights the importance of cultivating skills and knowledge to the point where you become invaluable as a trusted advisor or consultant. By leveraging automation and technology to handle mundane tasks, you can focus on developing your judgment and honing your ability to make sound decisions, which positions you for greater success and financial rewards.

19

If you're leveraged with capital, code, or people, and own equity, then good decisions have a much larger earning impact than hard work.

When you have leverage in the form of capital, code, or people, and you also have equity, the impact of making good decisions becomes much greater than simply working hard. It's like the power of compound interest in finance, but it applies to other aspects of life as well.

Think about it - when you have the resources and support to execute your ideas and make smart choices, the results can be exponential. It's not just about putting in long hours and working tirelessly; it's about making strategic moves that have a lasting and significant impact.

For example, in business, those who are trusted and have built strong relationships over time are given higher positions and responsibilities. Their reputation compounds, making them even more valuable. The same goes for your personal reputation - if you consistently build and maintain a positive reputation, it becomes immensely valuable in the long run.

So, rather than solely focusing on hard work, it is crucial to recognize the power of leverage and good decision-making in maximizing your earning potential and overall success.

20

Earn with your Mind. Not your time

Prioritize leveraging your intellectual abilities and knowledge to create wealth and success, rather than relying solely on trading your time for money. It emphasizes the importance of generating income through intellectual pursuits, such as developing innovative ideas, creating intellectual property, and acquiring valuable skills and expertise.

Rather than being limited by the number of hours in a day, earning with your mind allows for unlimited potential and possibilities. By continuously expanding our intellectual capital and investing in our personal growth, we can create sustainable and scalable earning opportunities that transcend traditional time-based income.

This quote challenges us to think beyond the conventional 9-to-5 mindset and explore ways to utilize our minds to generate lasting wealth and fulfillment. It reminds us that our intellectual capacity and the value we bring to the world can have a compounding effect, leading to long-term success and prosperity.

21

You don't get rich by spending your time to save money. You get rich by saving your time to make money

Focusing solely on saving money will not lead to wealth and success. Instead, the key to becoming rich is to prioritize and invest your time in activities that generate income and create opportunities for growth.

Saving time by efficiently managing tasks and delegating responsibilities allows you to focus on money-making activities such as building businesses, developing valuable skills, or investing in profitable ventures.

By understanding the value of time and directing it towards making money, you increase your chances of achieving financial prosperity. It's not about being frugal and trying to save every penny, but rather about being strategic and intentional with how you use your time to generate wealth.

22

Whenever you can in life, optimize for independence rather than pay. If you have independence and you're accountable on your output, as opposed to your input—that's the dream

In life, it's better to prioritize independence over a high salary. When you have independence, you're able to take ownership of your work and focus on the results you produce, rather than simply putting in hours.

This is the ultimate goal.

Instead of being tied down to a job where you're constantly trading your time for money, strive for freedom and the ability to work on your own terms. Independence gives you the power to make decisions and shape your own path. It allows you to be accountable for the outcomes you achieve and gives you the freedom to explore new opportunities. So, rather than chasing a paycheck, aim for independence and the ability to be in control of your own destiny. That's where true fulfillment lies.

23

A startup is a theory about something the market wants, but doesn't yet exist

A startup is like a hypothesis about what the market wants, but doesn't already have. It's like having an idea for a product or service that you believe people will really want and find value in, even if it doesn't currently exist. It's like seeing a gap in the market and coming up with a solution to fill that gap.

Imagine it like this: You have this theory, this belief that if you create something that meets a certain need or solves a specific problem, people will flock to it. They will want it, they will buy it, and it will become successful. But it's just a theory at this point, an unproven idea.

So, when you decide to start a startup, you're essentially taking a leap of faith. You're betting on your theory being right, on your idea being something that people will actually want. And if you're able to prove your theory correct, if you're able to create something that truly resonates with the market, then you have the potential for great success.

24

Pick an industry where you can play long term games with long term people

In life, it's important to choose an industry where you can engage in long-term relationships and partnerships. This means surrounding yourself with people who are committed to playing the long game, just like you.

When you find yourself in such an industry, you have the opportunity to build trust with others over time, which is crucial for success. Think about the top leaders and managers in high positions - they are entrusted with such responsibilities because their relationships and track record have compounded over the years.

By consistently displaying integrity and sticking to your commitments, you can compound not only your capital but also your reputation. Your reputation, if nurtured and maintained for decades, can become exponentially more valuable than someone who may be talented but doesn't prioritize long-term relationships.

25

If you want to start a tech company and aren't a maker, find a brilliant technologist and become their API to the rest of the world

Starting a tech company requires technical expertise that not everyone possesses. If you lack the necessary skills but still want to pursue this path, the key is to form a partnership with a brilliant technologist. In this partnership, your role will be to serve as the bridge between the technologist and the outside world, acting as their interface or "API" (Application Programming Interface).

This means that you will be responsible for communicating the brilliant technologist's ideas, innovations, and products to the rest of the world. You will play a crucial role in connecting the technologist's brilliance with potential customers, investors, and partners. By doing so, you enable the technologist to focus on what they do best – creating amazing technology – while you handle the external communications and relationships.

In essence, the big idea here is recognizing and leveraging your strengths and capabilities to build a successful tech company, even if you aren't the one with the technical expertise. Collaboration and complementary skills are key to unlocking the full potential of a startup.

26

You're never going to get rich renting out your time

Simply trading your time for money will never lead to long-term wealth. It emphasizes the importance of finding ways to leverage your time and efforts to create assets or opportunities that can generate income even when you're not actively working. Merely working as an employee or charging an hourly rate limits your earning potential because it relies solely on the hours you put in.

To truly accumulate wealth, you need to invest your time and energy into activities that have the potential to compound and grow over time. This could mean starting a business, investing in assets like stocks or real estate, or developing valuable skills that allow you to create products or services with scalable revenue streams.

By focusing on long-term strategies and finding ways to generate income beyond trading time for money, you increase your chances of achieving financial success.

27

Your goal in life is to find out the people who need you the most, to find out the business that needs you the most, to find the project and the art that needs you the most. There is something out there just for you

Our goal in life is to find our unique purpose and contribution to the world. It is about identifying the people, businesses, projects, and art that truly need us and where we can make the most impact.

Seek out those opportunities that align with our skills, passions, and values, rather than chasing superficial success or following societal expectations. It emphasizes the importance of finding our true calling and making a meaningful difference in the lives of others. Instead of searching for validation or trying to fit into predefined roles, we are urged to focus on discovering our authentic selves and finding the areas where we can bring value and fulfillment. Ultimately, there is something out there that is perfectly suited for each of us.

28

If you wanted to be rich in the 1800s you did it with Labour In the 1900s with Capital Now you do it with code

In the past, if you wanted to become rich, you would rely on manual labor in the 1800s or invest in capital in the 1900s. However, in today's world, the key to wealth lies in code.

This means that the ability to write and understand computer code has become extremely valuable and can lead to great financial success. With the rise of technology and the internet, coding skills have become essential for creating innovative products and services, building successful businesses, and even finding lucrative job opportunities. Code has become the new currency of wealth creation in our modern era.

29

Real wealth is created by starting your own companies or even by investing. In an investment firm, they're buying equity. These are the routes to wealth. It doesn't come through the hours

Real wealth isn't just about putting in the hours at a job, but rather about pursuing entrepreneurial ventures or making strategic investments. Starting your own company or investing in others' businesses allows you to acquire ownership and equity, ultimately leading to wealth.

Simply working long hours isn't enough to build substantial wealth. It's about taking calculated risks, building relationships, and making wise investment decisions. Building wealth also involves compounding, similar to the concept of compound interest. Just as interest grows over time, so does your reputation and trustworthiness.

By consistently delivering high-quality work and maintaining integrity, your reputation will compound and become incredibly valuable. In the long run, this can be more valuable than raw talent alone.

30

Technology democratizes consumption but consolidates production. The best person in the world for anything, gets to do it for everyone

Technology has revolutionized the way we consume, making it accessible and available to everyone. From streaming services to online shopping, we now have easy access to a wide range of products and services.

However, when it comes to production, technology has consolidated power in the hands of the best individuals. The most skilled and talented people in any field have the opportunity to create and produce for the entire population.

In simpler terms, this quote suggests that while technology has made consumption more democratic, with everyone being able to access and enjoy the same products, it has also concentrated the power of production in the hands of the most capable individuals.

These experts, the best of the best, are the ones who get to create and provide for all of us.

31

The most important skill for getting rich is becoming a perpetual learner. You have to know how to learn anything you want to learn

To get rich, you need to constantly be learning. It's not just about making money, but about expanding your knowledge and skills.

Learning is the key to unlocking opportunities and staying ahead in a competitive world. Whether it's learning about finance, business, technology, or any other field, the more you learn, the more you can apply that knowledge to make smart decisions and create wealth.

Being a perpetual learner means being open-minded, curious, and willing to adapt. It means seeking out new information, challenging your beliefs, and embracing lifelong growth.

32

Building a following on Twitter is building a castle out of sand, as the implacable tide shifts in and out. Invest in the free and open web - blogs, podcasts, newsletters

Focusing on building a strong and lasting online presence. While Twitter may provide instant gratification with its quick followers and likes, it is not a reliable foundation for long-term success.

Building a following on platforms that allow for more in-depth content creation, such as blogs, podcasts, and newsletters, creates a more solid and sustainable presence. These mediums provide an opportunity to showcase your expertise, establish trust with your audience, and cultivate a loyal following over time.

By investing in these channels, you can create a lasting impact and reach a broader audience, ultimately leading to greater success in the digital world.

33

Leverage is a force multiplier for your judgement

When you have leverage, it's like having a superpower. It amplifies the impact of your decisions and actions. Picture it like using a lever to move something heavy with much less effort than doing it by hand. Trust me, it makes a world of difference.

Think about it. If you have the ability to leverage resources, connections, or knowledge, your judgment becomes more potent. You can make smarter choices and achieve more significant results. For example, if you have access to key information or influential people, you can use that leverage to make informed decisions and create valuable opportunities.

Leverage is not just about having power, but using it effectively. It's like having a secret weapon in your arsenal. So, focus on building leverage in your life - whether it's through developing valuable skills, cultivating strong relationships, or gaining access to vital resources. Leverage can be the game-changer that propels you towards success.

34

Technology destroys jobs and replaces them with opportunities

Naval highlights the transformative power of technology in the job market. While technology may lead to the elimination of certain job roles, it also paves the way for the creation of new and different opportunities.

Think about it this way: when machines started replacing factory workers in the Industrial Revolution, many jobs were lost. However, this led to the emergence of new industries and job prospects in the technology sector. Similarly, advancements in automation and artificial intelligence may displace certain jobs today, but they also open up avenues in fields like data analysis, software development, and robotics.

The key idea here is that although technology may disrupt employment in the short term, it ultimately creates a cycle of destruction and creation. It is up to individuals to adapt and acquire the skills needed to seize the new opportunities that arise. So, rather than fearing the impact of technology, we should embrace it as a catalyst for progress and growth.

35

In any situation in life, you always have three choices: you can change it, you can accept it, or you can leave it

When faced with a situation, we ultimately have three options.

1. We can choose to change the situation by taking actions and making efforts to improve it. This requires us to identify what needs to be changed and actively work towards making those changes.
2. We can choose to accept the situation as it is. This means acknowledging that there are certain circumstances beyond our control and learning to embrace them. Acceptance requires us to adapt and find contentment within the given situation, without seeking to change it.
3. We can choose to leave the situation altogether. This means recognizing when a situation is not aligned with our values, goals, or well-being, and making the decision to move on. Leaving can be a difficult decision, but it allows us to prioritize our own happiness and growth.

36

The first rule of handling conflict is don't hang around with people who are constantly engaging in conflict

"The first rule of handling conflict is don't hang around with people who are constantly engaging in conflict." This quote by Naval Ravikant emphasizes the importance of choosing our company wisely when it comes to conflict. Conflict is a part of life, but surrounding ourselves with individuals who are constantly involved in conflicts can be draining and unproductive.

By avoiding these people, we create a healthier and more peaceful environment for ourselves. This doesn't mean avoiding conflict altogether, but rather ensuring that we are surrounded by individuals who prioritize resolution and growth over constant turmoil.

When we choose to associate with people who are not constantly engaged in conflict, we open ourselves up to positive and constructive relationships. These relationships foster personal and professional growth, as well as a sense of trust and support. Ultimately, by being selective about the company we keep, we can create a more harmonious and fulfilling life.

37

Wealth creation is an evolutionarily recent positive-sum game. Status is an old zero-sum game. Those attacking wealth creation are often just seeking status

The big idea behind this quote is that wealth creation is a relatively new concept in the grand scheme of human history, whereas the pursuit of status has been around for a long time. In today's society, many individuals attack wealth creation because they are actually seeking status rather than genuinely criticizing the process.

To put it simply, people attack the idea of creating wealth because they want to be seen as superior or important in the eyes of others. They may criticize successful individuals or point out flaws in the system as a way to elevate their own status. However, this quote suggests that true wealth creation is a positive-sum game, benefiting everyone involved, while seeking status is a zero-sum game where one person's gain is another person's loss.

In essence, Naval Ravikant is highlighting the importance of recognizing the motivations behind criticisms and understanding that wealth creation can be a mutually beneficial endeavor, contrary to what some may believe.

38

There is no skill called 'business.' Avoid business magazines and business classes

The big idea behind this quote is that "business" is not a specific skill or knowledge that can be learned from magazines or classes. Instead, it is a combination of various skills, relationships, and experiences that are built over time.

Naval Ravikant suggests that focusing too much on business magazines and classes can be misleading because they often promote short-term tactics or generic advice that may not be applicable to individual situations.

Instead, he emphasizes the importance of building long-term relationships, gaining real-world experience, and continuously learning and adapting. Success in business comes from a deep understanding of human behavior, effective communication, problem-solving, and the ability to navigate complex situations.

By avoiding the narrow focus on "business" and taking a holistic approach to personal growth and development, individuals can cultivate the skills and mindset necessary for long-term success in their professional pursuits.

39

Success is the inevitable byproduct of learning (not education)If the work doesn't require creativity, delegate it, automate it, or leave it

Success is often associated with formal education and the accumulation of degrees and qualifications. However, Naval Ravikant argues that true success comes from continuous learning rather than simply acquiring education. Learning is a lifelong process that goes beyond the confines of academic institutions. It involves a curiosity-driven approach, embracing new experiences, and a willingness to adapt and grow.

The big idea behind this quote is that success is not guaranteed by diplomas and certificates alone. It is the result of actively seeking knowledge, expanding one's perspectives, and applying that learning in practical ways. Success is not a finite destination but a continuous journey of personal development. By prioritizing learning, we open ourselves up to new opportunities, build expertise, and cultivate the skills needed to navigate an ever-changing world.

Whether in our careers, relationships, or personal endeavors, success is the natural outcome of ongoing education and the accumulation of wisdom through real-life experiences.

40

The most accountable people have singular, public, and risky brands: Oprah, Trump, Kanye, Elon

"The most accountable people have singular, public, and risky brands: Oprah, Trump, Kanye, Elon."

When I look at this quote from Naval Ravikant, what stands out to me is the emphasis on accountability and the power of personal branding. Naval highlights these four individuals - Oprah, Trump, Kanye, and Elon - who have all built remarkable reputations and achieved immense success in their respective fields.

What I gather from this quote is that having a strong and distinct brand, one that is public and potentially controversial, can be a significant factor in holding oneself accountable. When you establish a brand that is unique to you, you are directly accountable to that brand and the public image you have created.

However, Naval also implies that taking risks is essential in building such a brand. These individuals have all taken risks, put their ideas and beliefs out there, and faced criticism and backlash in their journeys to success.

In essence, the big idea behind this quote is that by cultivating a singular, public, and risky brand, individuals can not only hold themselves accountable, but also create opportunities for extraordinary achievements and impact.

41

If the work doesn't require creativity, delegate it, automate it, or leave it.

If the work you're doing doesn't require any creativity, then it's better to find a way to delegate it, automate it, or just leave it altogether.

This quote is all about recognizing the value of creativity and the power it holds. When you're able to bring your unique perspective and innovative ideas to the table, you can make a significant impact. On the other hand, tasks that don't require creativity can often be repetitive or mundane, and they don't allow you to fully express yourself or contribute in a meaningful way.

So instead of wasting your time on these tasks, it's better to find someone else who can handle it or automate the process so that you can focus your energy on the things that really matter. By doing this, you're prioritizing your creativity and maximizing your potential for success.

42

By the time someone else tells you their winning strategy, it's too late

Importance of being proactive and staying ahead of the game. If you rely on others to share their strategies with you, you will always be one step behind. Success comes from taking the initiative and finding your own unique path.

Don't wait for someone to hand you the answers; go out and discover them for yourself. By the time a strategy becomes public knowledge, it has likely been exploited by those who were ahead of the curve. To truly succeed, you need to be at the forefront, constantly innovating and evolving. So don't rely on others, be proactive, and create your own winning strategies before it's too late.

43

The reward for getting on the stage is fame. The price of fame is you can't get off the stage

Once you have achieved fame or a high level of success, it becomes difficult to escape its demands and expectations.

Think of it like being on a stage. When you step onto that stage and gain recognition, you may receive rewards such as attention, admiration, and opportunities. However, the price you pay for that fame is that you can no longer easily step off the stage and retreat into a private life. People will constantly expect you to perform, to be in the public eye, and to live up to the image they have of you.

This quote reminds us that fame comes with responsibilities and sacrifices. It implies that once you have achieved a certain level of prominence, you may feel trapped by the attention and pressure that comes along with it. It serves as a cautionary reminder to consider the consequences before pursuing or chasing after fame.

44

Selfless ideas spread the furthest

Selfless ideas spread the furthest because they tap into the power of genuine human connection. When we think about ideas that have had a lasting impact on society, they are often rooted in selflessness and a desire to uplift others. These ideas resonate with people on a deep level, evoking emotions and inspiring action.

Selfless ideas have the ability to transcend boundaries and bring people together. They ignite empathy and create a sense of unity among individuals who may have different backgrounds and perspectives. By focusing on the greater good rather than personal gain, selfless ideas have a universal appeal and can reach far and wide.

Furthermore, selfless ideas have a ripple effect. When we share these ideas with others, they are more likely to be embraced and passed on. People are drawn to ideas that have the potential to make a positive impact. The more selfless ideas are spread, the more they gain momentum and have the power to shape the world.

In a society that often emphasizes individual success and material gain, selfless ideas offer a refreshing alternative. They remind us of the importance of compassion, collaboration, and making a difference in the lives of others.

When we prioritize selflessness in our thoughts and actions, we not only contribute to the betterment of society but also cultivate a sense of fulfillment and purpose within ourselves.

45

Karma is just you, repeating your patterns, virtues, and flaws until you finally get what you deserve

Karma is like a tape that keeps playing your actions, good or bad, over and over again until you finally receive what you deserve. It's like a cycle of repeating patterns, both in your virtues and flaws. Whether it's kindness or selfishness, honesty or deceit, these actions keep coming back to you. It's not about some external force punishing or rewarding you, but rather the consequences of your own choices.

So, if you want to change what you get in life, you have to change what you put out into the world. Break free from negative patterns and cultivate positive ones. Only then will you start to see a shift in the outcome you receive. Remember, you create your own karma, so make it count.

46

Memento Mori. Ultimate failure is assured in all human activities. Where's the risk?

Think about it, mate. We're all gonna fail at some point, no matter what we do. It's just the way life works. So why are we so scared of taking risks? We're all gonna end up six feet under anyways, so we might as well go all in and do what we really want to do.

The big idea here is that failure is inevitable, my friend. It's a part of the game, no matter what game you're playing. So instead of playing it safe and avoiding risks, embrace them. Take chances, follow your passions, and see what happens. Because at the end of the day, when you're lying on your deathbed, you don't want to regret not taking those risks and going after what truly mattered to you.

So go on, mate. Embrace failure, take risks, and live life to the fullest. After all, where's the risk when ultimate failure is already assured?

47

The problem with genius is that you have to tolerate madness

Naval highlights the inherent connection between exceptional intelligence and mental instability.

It suggests that genius often comes at the cost of dealing with madness or eccentricity. While geniuses possess extraordinary intellect and skills that allow them to achieve remarkable feats, they often exhibit unconventional or erratic behavior that may be challenging for others to understand or accept. This quote emphasizes the need to accept and tolerate the idiosyncrasies and unconventional nature of genius in order to fully appreciate and benefit from their brilliance. It implies that to truly appreciate and benefit from genius, one must be willing to navigate the complexities and nuances of their minds, which may not conform to societal norms or expectations.

48

If you can't be happy with a coffee, you won't be happy with a yacht

If you can't find joy in the small, simple things in life, like having a cup of coffee, then you won't find happiness in extravagant and materialistic things, like owning a yacht.

The big idea behind this quote is that true happiness comes from within and isn't dependent on external possessions or achievements. It's about appreciating and finding contentment in the present moment, rather than constantly seeking for more or better things. Material possessions may bring temporary pleasure, but they won't sustain long-term happiness.

Developing an attitude of gratitude and learning to find joy in the little things can lead to a more fulfilling and satisfying life. It's a reminder to prioritize experiences, relationships, and inner fulfillment over material wealth.

49

Don't focus on more than one desire at a time

If you can't find joy in the small, simple things in life, like having a cup of coffee, then you won't find happiness in extravagant and materialistic things, like owning a yacht.

The big idea behind this quote is that true happiness comes from within and isn't dependent on external possessions or achievements. It's about appreciating and finding contentment in the present moment, rather than constantly seeking for more or better things. Material possessions may bring temporary pleasure, but they won't sustain long-term happiness. Developing an attitude of gratitude and learning to find joy in the little things can lead to a more fulfilling and satisfying life. It's a reminder to prioritize experiences, relationships, and inner fulfillment over material wealth.

50

Study logic and math, because once you've mastered them, you won't fear any book

When Naval says this, I believe he's highlighting the power of critical thinking and problem-solving skills.

Logic and math form the foundations of rational thinking and reasoning. When you're able to think logically and understand mathematical concepts, you develop a mental framework that allows you to tackle any kind of information or subject matter with confidence.

It's not about memorizing facts or specific knowledge, but about cultivating a mindset that enables you to analyze and break down complex ideas. By sharpening your logical and mathematical abilities, you build a solid intellectual toolkit that can be applied to any field or topic of interest. This quote encourages us to invest our time and effort in developing these fundamental skills, as they empower us to navigate the vast sea of knowledge without fear or intimidation.

51

You want to be rich and anonymous, not poor and famous

It is more desirable to be wealthy and maintain a sense of privacy rather than being poor but well-known. It emphasizes the importance of financial security and highlights the drawbacks of fame and public recognition.

Being rich provides the opportunity for financial freedom, comfort, and the ability to make choices without worrying about money. On the other hand, fame often comes with a loss of privacy and personal freedom, as one's life becomes open to public scrutiny.

The quote encourages individuals to prioritize financial success and the benefits it brings, rather than seeking fame or public attention. It suggests that being rich and anonymous allows for a better quality of life and the freedom to live on your own terms.

52

Once you've truly controlled your own fate, for better or for worse, you'll never let anyone else tell you what to do

Once you're in control of your own destiny, whether it turns out good or bad, you won't let others dictate your actions. It's about taking charge of your life, making your own decisions, and being responsible for the consequences.

When you've reached that point of true autonomy, you realize the immense power that comes with it. No longer will you allow anyone to tell you what to do or mold your path according to their desires. You become the architect of your own life, shaping it to align with your values and aspirations. This quote underscores the significance of self-determination and the freedom it brings. It empowers you to chart your own course and ensures that you never surrender that control to someone else.

53

Happiness without material comfort is playing on hard mode

Happiness without material comfort is like playing a difficult video game on expert mode. It's not impossible, but it definitely makes things harder. When you have the basic necessities and comforts in life, like a roof over your head, good food, and a bit of money in your pocket, it creates a foundation of stability and security.

It allows you to focus on higher level things like personal growth, relationships, and self-fulfillment. On the other hand, when you're constantly struggling to meet your basic needs, it becomes difficult to find happiness and contentment because your energy is consumed by survival mode. It's not to say that material comfort guarantees happiness, but it certainly makes the game of life a little easier to play.

54

Reading is faster than listening, doing is faster than watching

When we read, we can absorb knowledge much more quickly than if we were simply listening to someone speak. Similarly, when we take action and engage in activities, we learn and progress faster than if we were just passively observing others.

The big idea behind this quote is that active engagement accelerates our learning and growth. Instead of being passive consumers, we should strive to be active participants in our own lives. By reading and acquiring knowledge, we can expand our understanding and make informed decisions. Furthermore, by taking action and applying what we learn, we can actually see results and make progress towards our goals. This quote serves as a reminder to prioritize active learning and doing, rather than relying solely on passive forms of information consumption.

55

Persistence beats timing. Execution beats luck. Not immediately, but eventually

Persistence beats timing means that consistently putting in effort and working towards a goal is more important than waiting for the perfect opportunity to arise. It's about not giving up and staying committed even when things don't go as planned. Timing may have some influence, but it's not the deciding factor.

Execution beats luck indicating that taking action and actually doing the work is more crucial than relying purely on luck or chance.

It emphasizes the importance of putting in the effort, being proactive, and continuously improving. While immediate success may not always be guaranteed, if you persistently execute and stay committed, the desired outcome will eventually be achieved.

56

Desire is a contract that you make with yourself to be unhappy until you get what you want

Desire is a powerful force that can drive us to pursue our goals and dreams.

But this quote reminds us that desire comes with a price. When we desire something, we enter into a contract with ourselves, a promise to be unhappy until we attain what we want. We often think that achieving our desires will bring us happiness, but this mindset can lead to a perpetual state of dissatisfaction. It's important to understand that true happiness doesn't come from external circumstances or possessions.

Instead, it comes from within, from finding contentment in the present moment and appreciating what we already have. By releasing our attachment to desires and focusing on inner peace and gratitude, we can break the contract of unhappiness and find true joy in life.

57

Spend your time in the company of geniuses, sages, children, and books

Surround yourself with people who inspire you, who have wisdom to share, who see the world with fresh eyes, and with knowledge that lies in books. Let their presence in your life compound your growth, enrich your perspectives, and broaden your understanding of the world.

- Geniuses, with their brilliance, ignite a spark within you, pushing you to stretch your own limits.
- Sages, with their deep insights, offer you guidance and wisdom beyond measure.
- Children, with their innocence and curiosity, remind you to approach life with wonder and embrace new experiences.
- And books, oh the wonders they hold! They contain the accumulated knowledge, experiences, and wisdom of countless minds.

Immerse yourself in their pages to unlock new ideas and perspectives. Surrounding yourself with these four sources of inspiration will compound your own personal growth and illuminate your journey through life.

58

If your idea of money is what it was yesterday, you will lose it to the people who know what money will be tomorrow

If you think of money in the same way that you did yesterday, you will be left behind by those who understand how money will evolve in the future. Money is not a static concept, it is constantly evolving and changing. Those who are aware and adapt their understanding of money to keep up with these changes will be able to seize new opportunities and succeed financially.

To put it simply, if you cling to outdated beliefs about money and refuse to update your thinking, you will miss out on the potential to grow and accumulate wealth. Being open to new ideas and staying informed about emerging trends in the world of finance is crucial to staying ahead in the game.

So, don't get stuck in the past. Embrace the future of money and stay educated about its transformations, because that knowledge will be key to your financial success.

59

We study science to learn how to get what we want. We study philosophy to know what to want in the first place

When it comes to science, the purpose is to figure out how to achieve our desires. We learn the methods, strategies, and techniques to get what we want. On the other hand, philosophy helps us understand what we should actually want in the first place. It guides us to ponder and question our desires, values, and beliefs.

Philosophy delves into the deeper meaning of life, our purpose, and the nature of reality. Without philosophy, we might find ourselves pursuing goals that ultimately don't fulfill us or align with our true selves. By studying philosophy, we gain clarity on what truly matters to us, what brings us joy and fulfillment, and what values we want to prioritize. It steers us towards a life of meaning and purpose, guiding us towards the right path to happiness. So, science teaches us how to get what we want, but philosophy teaches us what we should want in the first place.

60

If you can't decide, the answer is No

If you find yourself unable to make a decision, the answer is simply no. This may seem counterintuitive, but it is a powerful principle to live by.

Indecision often stems from a lack of clarity or conviction. If you truly wanted something or believed in it, you would not hesitate to say yes. The inability to decide indicates that deep down, you are not fully committed or convinced. Making decisions is about taking a stand and owning your choices. Saying no allows you to prioritize your time, energy, and resources.

It helps you avoid half-hearted commitments and enables you to focus on what truly matters to you.

61

Learning is cheap, education is expensive

Learning is the process of gaining knowledge or skills, and it doesn't have to be expensive. There are many resources available for free or at a low cost that can help us learn new things. On the other hand, education refers to the formal system of acquiring knowledge, which often comes with a high price tag. Going to college, obtaining degrees, and getting certifications can be costly endeavors.

The big idea behind this quote is that education, in the traditional sense, can be a significant investment in terms of time, money, and effort. However, learning, the act of continuously acquiring knowledge and skills, is something that can be done at a lower cost. It emphasizes the importance of lifelong learning and the idea that education shouldn't be limited to formal institutions. With the abundance of information and resources available today, we have the opportunity to educate ourselves beyond the confines of traditional education systems.

62

Read the books they want to ban.

This quote is all about challenging the status quo and expanding your knowledge beyond the boundaries set by society. It encourages you to explore ideas and perspectives that may be controversial or unpopular, because they often contain valuable insights and truths that are being suppressed.

By reading the banned books, you gain a deeper understanding of different viewpoints, cultures, and historical events, allowing you to form your own opinions and think critically. It's about seeking out knowledge that may be uncomfortable or challenging, because that's where growth and learning happen. By not limiting ourselves to what is deemed acceptable or popular, we open ourselves up to a wealth of information and ideas that can help us navigate the complexities of life and make more informed decisions. So, embrace the banned books and expand your mind.

63

The highest status people in human history are those that asked for nothing and gave everything

The most esteemed individuals throughout history are those who lived a selfless life, contributing without expecting anything in return. These people embody true greatness by demonstrating kindness, empathy, and generosity. Rather than seeking personal gains or recognition, they prioritize the well-being and happiness of others.

This quote highlights the notion that achieving a high status in society is not dependent on wealth, fame, or power, but rather on the ability to make a significant and positive impact on the lives of those around them. It suggests that true fulfillment and success come from selfless acts and genuine care for others.

By selflessly giving and expecting nothing in return, individuals can leave a lasting legacy and be truly revered in the annals of human history.

64

Life hack: When in bed, meditate. Either you will have a deep meditation, or fall asleep. Victory either way

When you're lying in bed, unsure of what to do, try meditating. It's like a life hack. You have two possible outcomes - either you'll have a deep meditation session and gain inner peace, or you'll just fall asleep and have a good rest.

Either way, it's a victory. Sometimes we get caught up in the hustle and bustle of life, and we forget to take a pause, to connect with ourselves. Meditating before sleep can be a way to calm our minds and find a sense of tranquility. It doesn't require any special skills or techniques, just the willingness to be present with your thoughts and emotions.

65

If you're leveraged with capital, code, or people, and own equity, then good decisions have a much larger earning impact than hard work

If you have borrowed money, hired talented people, or have ownership in a business, then making smart decisions will have a bigger impact on your earnings than just working hard. Hard work is important, but it's not enough to guarantee success. Making good decisions means strategically using the resources you have to maximize your earning potential.

For example, if you have borrowed money to start a business, making the right decisions about how to use that money can lead to higher profits. Similarly, if you have a team of talented employees, making good decisions about how to utilize their skills and knowledge can lead to greater success. If you have ownership in a business, making wise choices about how to grow and expand that business can result in significant financial gains.

In short, working hard is necessary, but being strategic and making smart decisions is what truly drives success and financial growth.

66

Changing habits: Pick one thing. Cultivate a desire. Visualize it.

> Changing habits: Pick one thing. Cultivate a desire. Visualize it. Plan a sustainable path. Identify needs, triggers, and substitutes. Tell your friends. Track meticulously. Self-discipline is a bridge to a new self-image. Bake in the new self-image. It's who you are, now

Changing habits is a process that requires focus and discipline. To start, pick one specific habit you want to change and cultivate a deep desire to make that change. Visualize yourself embodying that change and plan a sustainable path to achieve it. Along the way, identify the needs, triggers, and substitutes related to the habit, so you can better manage them.

Share your goal with your friends and hold yourself accountable. Tracking your progress meticulously will help you stay on track and measure your success. As you consistently practice the new habit, it will become a part of your self-image.

This transformed self-image will shape your identity and become who you truly are. By following these steps, you can successfully change your habits and become the person you aspire to be.

67

Money doesn't buy happiness - it buys freedom

Money alone can't bring us true happiness or fulfillment in life. It's not about accumulating material possessions or chasing endless wealth. Instead, money provides us with the freedom to make choices and pursue our passions. It allows us to have more control over our lives and the ability to do what we truly enjoy.

Money gives us the power to say "yes" to experiences and opportunities that align with our values and desires. It's not about the money itself, but the freedom it brings to create a life that is meaningful and fulfilling.

68

It isn't 10,000 hours that creates outliers, it's 10,000 iterations

The key to achieving exceptional success is not solely through the accumulation of a certain number of hours practicing or training, but rather through a focus on continuous improvement and refinement over a large number of iterations or attempts.

In other words, reaching an expert level or becoming an outlier in a particular field is not solely dependent on putting in a set amount of time, but rather on pushing oneself to learn, adapt, and refine their approach through repeated iterations. It emphasizes the importance of being persistent, adaptable, and open to feedback and growth.

By embracing a mindset of constant iteration and improvement, individuals can reach exceptional levels of skill or success, surpassing the traditional idea of mastery-based purely on the accumulation of hours.

69

You'll do better work if you're bored rather than busy

When you're constantly busy, it's easy to think that you're being productive and getting things done. However, Naval suggests that being bored leads to better work.

Think about it this way: when you're busy, your mind is preoccupied with multiple tasks and you're always on the go. This leaves little room for deep thinking, creative problem-solving, and reflection.

On the other hand, when you're bored, your mind has the opportunity to wander and explore new ideas. It allows you to tap into your creativity and come up with innovative solutions.

Being bored also gives you the chance to truly focus on the task at hand without distractions. You can invest your full attention and energy into your work, leading to higher quality and more meaningful results.

So, instead of embracing busyness, embrace moments of boredom. Embrace the opportunity to slow down, let your mind wander, and engage in deep work. It's in these moments that you'll find the space to do your best work.

70

Before you search for product/market fit, make sure your passion/product fit. It's a long journey

"BE PASSIONATE ABOUT YOUR PRODUCT BEFORE YOU SEEK SUCCESS IN THE MARKET"

Being genuinely passionate about your product or idea before diving into the pursuit of product/market fit. Naval suggests that the journey to success is a long and challenging one, and having a genuine passion for what you are creating will help you stay committed and dedicated throughout.

Passion provides the fuel that keeps you going when faced with obstacles, setbacks, and failures. It is the driving force behind your perseverance, creativity, and resilience. Without a true passion for your product, it becomes easy to lose interest and motivation, especially during difficult times.

By focusing on passion/product fit first, you ensure that you are genuinely invested in what you are creating. This deep connection and enthusiasm will not only help you navigate the challenges that come with building a successful product but will also resonate with customers and potential investors who are drawn to your authenticity and dedication.

71

A vacation is a very expensive way to schedule the time to read a book in peace

Taking a vacation may seem like a luxurious way to unwind and relax, but if you think about it, it's a very expensive way to set aside time to read a book without interruptions. When you go on vacation, you're spending money on travel, accommodation, and other expenses just to find a peaceful environment for reading.

We often need to invest a significant amount of resources to create the circumstances that allow us to fully enjoy simple pleasures like reading. Instead of going on an expensive vacation, we can find ways to carve out uninterrupted time in our everyday lives to indulge in leisure activities.

By eliminating unnecessary expenses and distractions, we can prioritize the things that bring us joy and enrich our minds without breaking the bank. It reminds us to value the simplicity in life and find contentment in the little things, rather than relying on extravagant experiences for tranquility.

72

The best jobs are neither decreed nor degreed. They are creative expressions of continuous learners in free markets

The big idea behind the quote is that the most fulfilling and successful jobs are not determined by degrees or external validation, but rather by individuals who are continuously learning and expressing their creativity in free markets.

Naval suggests that true satisfaction and success in one's career come from actively seeking knowledge and growth, rather than relying solely on formal education or credentials. He emphasizes the importance of adaptability, creativity, and a thirst for knowledge in thriving within the ever-changing dynamics of free markets. By embracing continuous learning and being open to new ideas and opportunities, individuals can carve out unique and fulfilling paths for themselves in their professional lives.

73

Asymmetric opportunities: Invest in startups. Start a company. Create a book, podcast, or video. Create a (software) product. Go on many first dates. Go to a cocktail party. Read a Lindy book. Move to a big city. Buy Bitcoin. Tweet

Opportunities are everywhere, but they are not all created equal.

Look for the ones that have an unfair advantage, where the potential payoff is much greater than the effort you put in. Investing in startups, starting your own company, creating content like books, podcasts, or videos, developing a software product, going on many first dates, attending networking events, expanding your knowledge by reading influential books, moving to a big city for more opportunities, investing in Bitcoin, and using social media platforms like Twitter all have the potential to offer asymmetric rewards.

In simpler terms, these are the things that can give you a lot more than what you invest. The key is to be open to exploring various avenues and taking calculated risks. By being proactive and seizing these opportunities, you increase your chances of finding that one thing that has the potential to change your life dramatically.

74

The really smart thinkers are clear thinkers. They understand the basics at a very, very fundamental level

Smart thinkers are those who have a clear understanding of the basics at a fundamental level. It's not about being an expert in complex theories or using fancy jargon. Instead, it's about grasping the foundational principles of a subject and being able to simplify and communicate them effectively. When you truly understand the basics, you can build upon them with confidence and navigate through any challenges that may arise.

By focusing on the fundamentals, you gain clarity and avoid getting lost in unnecessary complexity. It's like having a solid foundation for a house - without it, the structure becomes weak and unstable. Similarly, in our pursuit of knowledge and problem-solving, a strong understanding of the basics allows us to think critically, make informed decisions, and ultimately find effective solutions.

75

AI will replace the people who think it will

AI, or artificial intelligence, has been a topic of discussion and speculation for a while now. Some people fear that AI will replace humans in various fields, taking away their jobs and rendering their skills useless. However, this quote by Naval Ravikant suggests a different perspective.

According to Naval, those who believe that AI will replace humans are the ones who will be replaced. This implies that instead of fearing and being complacent, we should adapt and evolve with the changing times. Instead of clinging stubbornly to our current roles and skills, we should constantly learn, grow, and seek new opportunities.

The big idea behind this quote is that change is inevitable, and those who embrace it rather than resist it will thrive. Instead of being passive observers, we should actively participate and embrace the possibilities that AI and other technological advancements bring. By doing so, we can stay ahead of the game and continue to contribute in meaningful ways.

76

The single most important decision you make is where you live. It drives your business opportunities, relationships, food and water supply, politics, activities, and day-to-day quality of life

The decision of where you choose to live has a significant impact on various aspects of your life. It goes beyond just having a place to stay and affects your business opportunities, relationships, access to food and water, political environment, activities, and overall quality of life on a day-to-day basis.

This decision shapes the options available to you and can greatly influence your chances of success or fulfillment in different areas. By carefully considering the location where you live, you can optimize your surroundings to align with your goals and preferences, leading to a more satisfying and prosperous life.

77

All modern diseases are diseases of abundance. We punish ourselves by constantly entertaining our minds and bodies

In today's world of excess and abundance, we find ourselves constantly indulging and entertaining our minds and bodies. This never-ending pursuit of more, whether it be material possessions, information, or experiences, has led to the rise of modern diseases. We punish ourselves by overloading our minds with an overwhelming amount of stimuli, constantly seeking new forms of entertainment and distraction.

Similarly, our bodies suffer from the consequences of excessive consumption and sedentary lifestyles. We have become slaves to our desires and impulses, neglecting the importance of balance and moderation. To truly thrive and find contentment, we must break free from this self-imposed punishment and learn to embrace simplicity, mindful choices, and a conscious approach to our physical and mental well-being.

78

If you can neither give happiness nor receive it

Happiness is not just about receiving it from others, but also about being able to give it to others.

It's a two-way street. When you are able to bring joy and positivity into someone else's life, it not only enhances their well-being but also brings a sense of fulfillment and purpose to yourself.

Similarly, when you are open to receiving happiness from others, you allow yourself to experience the beauty and joy that they have to offer. It's about creating a cycle of giving and receiving happiness, which ultimately contributes to a more meaningful and contented life.

79

It doesn't take money to make money, it takes leverage to make money

Money alone is not enough to make more money. What you really need is leverage. Leverage means finding ways to multiply or increase your resources or abilities in order to achieve greater results. It's like using a lever to lift something heavy - you're using a small force to create a much larger impact.

This concept applies not just to money, but also to business relationships and your reputation. Building strong business relationships and maintaining a good reputation takes time and consistency. It's about sticking with it, doing good work, and earning people's trust. By doing this, you compound the value of your relationships and reputation over time.

So, the big idea behind this quote is that in order to make money and achieve success, you need to go beyond just having money and focus on leveraging your resources, relationships, and reputation to create greater opportunities and outcomes.

A Request

Thank you again for purchasing and reading this book. If you enjoyed it, can I ask for a quick favor?

As a self-published author, I rely heavily on Amazon reviews. If you could take 60 seconds to write an honest review, it would mean the world to me.

Any questions? Feel free to email me at shehraj@shehraj.com.

I appreciate your support!

About the Author

Hi, My name is Shehraj, I'm a content creator who loves to talk about books, business, lessons i learn from giants like Naval. Is this something you're interested in?

Feel free to connect with me on these platform

You can connect with me on:

🌐 https://shehraj.com

🐦 https://twitter.com/ishehraj

Subscribe to my newsletter:

✉ https://pageturnerpicks.substack.com